Scottish Wit and Wisdom

First published in 2007 by

Appletree Press Ltd
The Old Potato Station
14 Howard Street South
Belfast BT7 1AP

Tel: +44 (028) 90 24 30 74
Fax: +44 (028) 90 24 67 56
Email: reception@appletree.ie
Web: www.appletree.ie

Copyright © Appletree Press, 2007
Text by J.D. Sutherland
Photographs as acknowledged on page 92

A catalogue record for this book is available form the British Library.

Scottish Wit and Wisdom

ISBN: 978 1 84758 008 5

Desk & Marketing Editor: Jean Brown
Copy-editing: Jim Black and Laura Armstrong
Photographic Research: Laura Armstrong
Designer: Stuart Wilkinson
Production Manager: Paul McAvoy

9 8 7 6 5 4 3 2 1

AP3415

Scottish Wit and Wisdom

J.D. Sutherland

Scotland's National Emblem

Contents

Scottish Heather

Introduction

The Scots have always been known for possessing opinions, and a definite attitude to life. This does not automatically make them a quotable people, but many Scots have been gifted with the ability to turn a complex thought into a memorable epigram. This little volume offers a selection culled from among Scotland's greatest thinkers and writers, and others less celebrated. Some of the many pithy remarks in this book have been made by that most perceptive of social observers, Anonymous, and these have also been included. Other quotes and observations about the Scots have come from outsiders but are no less entertaining for their insight into the Scottish psyche. A final touch of savour is provided by some of the stranger or more outrageous traditional mottoes associated with particular clans and families.

Arthur's Seat, Edinburgh

The Land

Gae bring my guid auld harp aince mair;
Gae bring it free and fast,
For I maun sing another sang
Ere a' my glee is past;
And trow ye as I sing, my lads,
The burthen o't shall be -
Auld Scotland's howes and Scotland's knowes,
And Scotland's hills for me!

I drink a cup to Scotland yet,
Wi' a' the honours three!

Henry Riddell (1798-1870)

Scotland, thy mountains, thy valleys and fountains
Are famous in story – the birthplace of song.

Alexander Crawford

This is my country
The land that begat me,
These windy spaces
Are surely my own

Alexander Gray (1882-1968)

Rainy Day in Scotland

So this is your Scotland. It is rather nice, but dampish and Northern and one shrinks a trifle under one's skin. For these countries, one should be amphibian.

D.H. Lawrence (1858-1930)

Scotland is the country above all others that I have seen, in which a man of imagination may carve out his own pleasures; there are so many inhabited solitudes.

Dorothy Wordsworth (1771-1855)

Once you get the hang of it, and apprehend the type, it is a most beautiful and admirable little country – fit, for distinction etc., to make up a trio with Italy and Greece.

Henry James (1843-1916)

Did not strong connections draw me elsewhere, I believe Scotland would be the country I should choose to end my days in.

Benjamin Franklin (1706-1790)

Where's the coward that would not dare
To fight for such a land!

Sir Walter Scott (1771-1832)

Give me but one hour of Scotland –
Let me see it ere I die!

W.E. Aytoun (1813-1865)

And well know within that bastard land
Hath wisdom's goddess never held command…
Whose thistle well betrays the niggard earth,
Emblem of all to whom the land gives birth:
Each genial influence nurtured to resist:
A land of meanness, sophistry, and mist.

Lord Byron (1788-1824)

When shall I see Scotland again? Never shall I forget
the happy days I passed there, amidst odious smells,
barbarian sounds, bad suppers, excellent hearts, and
most enlightened and cultivated understanding.

Sydney Smith (1771-1845)

Edinburgh Castle

Dancing with Swords

The People

The Scots have been distinguished for humour – not for venomous wit, but for kindly, genial humour, which half loves what it laughs at – and this alone shows clearly enough that those to whom it belongs have not looked too exclusively on the gloomy side of the world.

James Anthony Froude (1818-1894)

The whole nation hitherto has been void of wit and humour, and even incapable of relishing it.

Horace Walpole (1717-1794)

The Scot is very much what I choose to call a secret humorist. He quietly creates his wit and jokes as if they were an unpermitted diversion, frowned on by the authorities.

Gordon Irving

Nowhere beats the heart so kindly
As beneath the tartan plaid.

W.E. Aytoun (1813-1865)

If the Scots knew enough to go indoors when it rained, they would never get any exercise.

Simeon Ford (1855-1933)

Scotsmen take all they can get, and a little more if they can.

Lord Advocate Maitland (1792-1851)

Trust yow no Skott.

Andrew Board (*c*. 1536)

Much may be made of a Scotsman, if he be caught young.

Samuel Johnson (1709-1784)

As Dr Johnson never said, Is there any Scotsman without charm?

J.M. Barrie (1860-1937)

I do indeed come from Scotland, but I cannot help it.
James Boswell (1740-1795)
That, Sir, I find, is what a very great many of your countrymen cannot help.
Samuel Johnson (1709-1795)

I have been trying all my life to like Scotchmen, and am obliged to desist from the experiment in despair.

Sydney Smith (1771-1845)

In all companies it gives me pleasure to declare that the English, as a people, are very little inferior to the Scots.

John Wilson (1785-1854)

This is certainly a fine country to grow old in. I could not spare a look to the young people, so much was I engrossed in contemplating their grandmothers.

Ann Grant

People imagine we Scots are all red-haired and about five feet small. It's fantastic. I reckon there's no race more romantic than the Scots.

Sean Connery (born 1930)

Grouse

The truth is that we are at bottom the most sentimental and emotional people on earth.

John Buchan (1875-1940)

English grouse are to Scotch what Scotchmen are to Englishmen. They are much more wary and provident birds, more given to locomotion.

Sir Robert Peel (1788-1850)

The Scotch are great charmers, and sing through their noses like musical tea-kettles.

Virginia Woolf (1882-1941)

Why do you softly, richly speak?
Rhythm so sweetly scanned?
Poverty hath the Gaelic and Greek
In my land.

Rachel Annand Taylor 'The Princess of Scotland' (1876-1960)

One cannot but be conscious of an underlying melancholy in Scotswomen. This melancholy is particularly attractive in the ballroom, where it gives a singular piquancy to the enthusiasm and earnestness they put into their national dances.

Stendhal [Marie-Henri Beyle] (1783-1842)

Put even the plainest woman into a beautiful dress and unconsciously she will try to live up to it.

Lady Duff Gordon (1863-1935)

And the difficultest job a man can do,
Is to come it brave and meek with thirty bob a week,
And feel that that's the proper thing for you.

John Davidson (1857-1909)

I like to tell people when they ask 'Are you an native born?' 'No sir, I am a Scotchman,' and I feel as proud as I am sure every Roman did when it was their boast to say 'I am a Roman citizen'.

Andrew Carnegie (1835-1919)

I am learning to live close to the lives of my friends without ever seeing them.

John Muir (1838-1914)

Friends are lost by calling often, and calling seldom.

Anonymous

The chain of friendship, however bright, does not stand the attrition of close contact.

Sir Walter Scott (1771-1832)

It's not lost what a friend gets.

Anonymous

It was a common saying, "The first tale by the goodman, and tales to daylight by the guest".

Hector Urquhart

Scottish Loch

Contentment in Scotland

The world is so full of a number of things,
I am sure we should all be as happy as kings.

Robert Louis Stevenson (1850-1894)

This is where the children of honest poverty have the
most precious of all advantages over those of wealth.
The mother, nurse, cook, governess, teacher, saint,
all in one; the father, exemplar, guide, counsellor and
friend! Thus were my brother and I brought up. What
has the child of a millionaire or nobleman that counts
compared to such a heritage?

Andrew Carnegie (1835-1919)

We can't for a certainty tell
What mirth may molest us on Monday,
But at least to begin the week well,
We can all be unhappy on Sunday.

Lord Neaves (1800-1876)

It is now the duty of the Scottish genius
Which has provided the economic freedom for it
To lead in the abandonment of creeds and moral
compromises
Of every sort

Hugh MacDiarmid (1892-1978)

Consumption is the sole end and purpose of production; and the interest of the producer ought to be attended to only so far as it may be necessary for promoting that of the consumer.

Adam Smith (1723-1790)

I cannot praise the Doctor's eyes,
I never saw his glance divine;
He always shuts them when he prays,
And when he preaches, he shuts mine.

George Outram (1805-1856)

God forbid that I should go to any heaven in which there are no horses.

R.B. Cunninghame Graham (1852-1936)

To live in hearts we leave behind
Is not to die.

Thomas Campbell (1777-1844)

A man with God is always in the majority.

John Knox (c. 1513-1572)

The principal part of faith is patience.

George Macdonald (1824-1905)

This little life is all we must endure,
The grave's most holy peace is ever sure,
We fall asleep and never wake again.

James Thomson (1834-1882)

Man's unhappiness, as I construe, comes of his
Greatness; it is because there is an Infinite in him,
which with all his cunning he cannot quite bury under
the Finite.

Thomas Carlyle (1795-1881)

Better keep the devil out, than have to put him out.

Anonymous

Madness need not be all breakdown. It may also be
breakthrough.

R.D. Laing (1927-1989)

My heart is a lonely hunter, that hunts on a lonely hill.

Fiona MacLeod (1856-1905)

Contented wi' little, and cantie wi' mair.

Robert Burns (1759-1796)

In the Highlands

It is perhaps a more fortunate destiny to have a taste for collecting shells than to be born a millionaire.

Robert Louis Stevenson (1850-1894)

Give a man a pipe he can smoke,
Give a man a book he can read,
And his home is bright with a calm delight,
Though the rooms be poor indeed.

James Thomson (1834-1882)

O grant me, Heaven, a middle state,
Neither too humble, nor too great;
More than enough for nature's ends,
With something left to treat my friends.

David Mallet (1705-1765)

It grows near the seashore, on banks, in clefts, but above all on the little green braes bordered with hazel-woods. It rarely reaches more than two feet in height, is neither white nor cream so much as old ivory; unassuming, modest, and known as the white rose of Scotland.

Neil M. Gunn (1891-1973)

Princes and lords are but the breath of kings:
An honest man's the noblest work o' God.

Robert Burns (1759-1796)

It takes a wise man to handle a lie.
A fool had better remain honest.

Norman Douglas (1868-1952)

Oh, what a tangled web we weave,
When first we practise to deceive.

Sir Walter Scott (1771-1832)

But Lord, remember me and mine
Wi' mercies temporal and divine,
That I for grace and gear may shine
Excelled by none;
And all the glory shall be thine,
Amen, Amen!

Robert Burns (1759-1796)

Burns of all poets is the most a Man.

Dante Gabriel Rossetti (1828-1882)

I that in heill was and in gladnes
Am trublit now with great seiknes,
And feblit with infirmitie
Timor mortis conturbat me

William Dunbar (*c.* 1465-1530)

But pleasures are like poppies spread,
You seize the flow'r, its bloom is shed;
Or like the snow falls in the river,
A moment white – then melts forever.

Robert Burns (1759-1796)

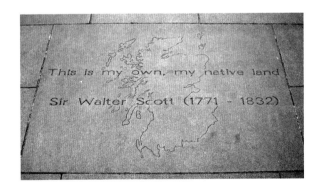

This is my own, my native land

Sir Walter Scott (1771 - 1832)

Whisky Barrels

The Spirit of Scotland

Freedom and whisky gang thegither –
Tak' aff your dram!

Robert Burns (1759-1796)

Single malts must be drunk with circumspection.
Contrary to the old joke about the Highlander liking
two things to be naked, one of them whisky, malts are
best drunk with a little water to bring out the aroma
and flavour.

Neil M. Gunn (1891-1973)

If it was raining, it was 'We'll have a dram to keep out
the wet'; if it was cold, 'We'll have a dram to keep
out the cold'; and if it was a fine day why then, 'We'll
drink its health.'

J.A. MacCulloch

The cure for which there is no disease

John Ferguson

The French drink all the time and kill their livers; the
Scots drink in bouts, and kill their neighbours.

Sir John Crofton

'... In a wee but-and-ben'

The Scotch do not drink… During the whole of two
or three pleasant weeks spent lecturing in Scotland,
I never on any occasion saw whisky made use of as
a beverage. I have seen people take it, of course,
as a medicine, or as a precaution, or as a wise
offset against a rather treacherous climate; but as a
beverage, never.

Stephen Leacock (1869-1944)

Moderation, sir, aye. Moderation is my rule. Nine or
ten is reasonable refreshment, but after that it's apt to
degenerate into drinking.

Anonymous

Just a wee deoch an doruis,
Just a wee drop, that's a';
Just a wee deoch an doruis,
Afore ye gang awa'.
There's a wee wifie waitin'
In a wee but-and-ben;
But if ye can say 'It's a braw bricht moonlicht nicht',
it's a' richt, ye ken.

Sir Harry Lauder (1870-1950)

A glass of wine is a glorious creature, and it reconciles poor humanity to itself; and that is what few things can do.

Sir Walter Scott (1771-1832)

The Scots invented golf, it's said,
And also good malt whisky;
If wearied when the first is played,
The other keeps them frisky.

Anonymous

Places in Scotland

The Hebrides…
There is still peace though not for me and not
Perhaps for long – still peace on the bevel hills
For those who can live as their fathers lived
On those islands.

Louis MacNeice (1907-1963)

Iona of my heart, Iona of my love, instead of monks'
voices shall be lowing of cattle, but ere the world
comes to an end, Iona shall be as it was.

St Columba (543-615)

Beautiful, glorious Scotland has spoiled me for every
other country.

Mary Todd Lincoln (1818-1862)

Aberdeen impresses the stranger as a city of granite
palaces, inhabited by people as definite as their
building material.

H.V. Morton (1892-1979)

Edinburgh

Ye lover of the picturesque, if ye wish to drown your
    grief,
Take my advice and visit the ancient town of Crieff.

William McGonagall (1825-1902)

I am glad to have seen the Caledonian Canal, but
don't want to see it again.

Matthew Arnold (1822-1888)

Dundee... As men have made it, it stands today
perhaps the completest monument in the entire
continent of human folly, avarice and selfishness.

Fionn McColla (1906-1975)

The impression Edinburgh has made on me is very
great; it is quite beautiful, totally unlike anything else
I have ever seen; and what is even more, Albert, who
has seen so much, says it is unlike anything he ever
saw.

Queen Victoria (1819-1901)

Who indeed, that has once seen Edinburgh, with its
couchant lion crag, but must see it again in dreams,
waking or sleeping?

Charlotte Brontë (1816-1855)

Urquhart Castle, Loch Ness

To none but those who have themselves suffered the thing in the body, can the gloom and depression of our Edinburgh winters be brought home.

Robert Louis Stevenson (1850-1894)

Most of the denizens wheeze, snuffle and exude a sort of snozzling whnoff whnoff, apparently through a hydrophile sponge.

Ezra Pound (1885-1972)

As we looked towards the castle, the little girl pointed out a black thing in the water and asked if it was a rock, but the object began to move and soon set off at a high speed to Lochend. We left the car and climbed down to the water's edge. A v-shaped wash was clearly seen, and a whole foaming wake, like that caused by a motor boat.

Lady Maud Baillie (in 1950)

The side was steep, the bottom deep,
From bank to bank the waters pouring;
The bonnie lass did quake for fear:
She heard the water kelpie roaring.

Border Ballad

The great thing about the way Glasgow is now is that if there is a nuclear attack it'll still look exactly the same afterwards.

Billy Connolly (born 1942)

Isna Embro a glorious city!

James Hogg (1770-1835)

Glasgow, that damned sprawling evil town

G.S. Fraser (1915-1980)

Abbotsford… That it should have been lived in is the most astonishing, staggering, saddening thing of all. Surely the saddest and strangest monument that Scott's genius created.

Edwin Muir (1887-1959)

'Heaven seems vera little improvement on Glesga,' a Glasgow man is said to have murmured, after death, to a friend who had predeceased him. 'Man, this is no' Heaven,' the other replied.

Anonymous

I will arise now, and go to Inverness,
And a small villa rent there, of lath and plaster built;
Nine bedrooms will I have there, and I'll don my native
    dress,
And walk around in a damned loud kilt.

Harry Graham (1874-1936)
after W.B. Yeats

From the lone sheiling on the misty island
Mountains divide us, and a waste of seas –
Yet still the blood is true, the heart is Highland,
And we in dreams behold the Hebrides.

Anonymous Canadian Boat Song

Speak well of the Hielands, but live in the laigh.

Old proverb

In spite of the difference of blood and language, the
Lowlander finds himself the sentimental countryman
of the Highlander.

Robert Louis Stevenson (1850-1894)

Ben Nevis, highest mountain in Scotland

Or whether the blood be Highland or Lowland or no
Or whether the skin be white or black as the sloe…
If only the heart beat true to the lilt of the song.

Air Fa La La La: Hebridean song

He who first met the Highlands swelling blue,
Will love each peak that shows a kindred hue,
Hail in each crag a friend's familiar face,
And clasp the mountain in his mind's embrace.

Lord Byron (1788-1824)

Scottish Hillside

Love in a Cold Climate

Ye're a bonny lad, and I'm a lassie free,
Ye're welcomer to tak' me than to let me be.

Allan Ramsay (1686-1758)

The white bloom of the blackthorn, she;
The small sweet raspberry blossom, she;
More fair the shy, rare glance of her eye
Than the world's wealth to me.

From the Gaelic

For there's nae luck about the house,
There's nae luck at a';
There's little pleasure in the house
When our gudeman's awa'.

Anonymous

Give me the highest joy
That the heart o' man can frame:
My bonnie, bonnie lassie,
When the kye come hame.

James Hogg (1770-1835)

Solway Firth

Love is ane fervent fire,
Kindlit without desire

Alexander Scott (1525-1584)

Love swells like the Solway, but ebbs like its tide.

Sir Walter Scott (1771-1832)

Love of our neighbour is the only door out of the
dungeon of self.

George Macdonald (1824-1905)

Follow love, and it will flee;
Flee it, and it follows ye.

Anonymous

As fair art thou, my bonnie lass,
So deep in luve am I;
And I will luve thee still, my dear,
Till a' the seas gang dry.

Robert Burns (1759-1796)

Marriage is a wonderful invention, but then again, so
is the bicycle repair kit.

Billy Connolly (born 1942)

Scottish Ceilidh

And for bonnie Annie Laurie
I'd lay me doun and dee.

William Douglas (1672-1748)

Yes, I have died for love, as others do;
But praised be God, it was in such a sort
That I revived within an hour or two.

Sir Robert Ayton (1570-1638)

Lord Rosebery sat by his fireside,
Beside his bonny leddy:
'Shall we dae the thing ye ken,
Or shall we hae our dinner?'
'As my lord pleases', said she then –
'But dinner isna ready'.

Anonymous

Skirl of the Pipes

National Pastimes

I will nae priest for me shall sing,
Nor yet nae bells for me to ring,
But ae Bag-pipe to play a spring.

Walter Kennedy (1460-1508)

I asked the piper: 'How long does it take to learn to play a
pibroch?'
He answered: 'It takes seven years to learn to play the
pipes, and seven years to learn to play a pibroch. And
then you need the poetry'.

George Bruce (1909-2002)

There sat Auld Nick, in shape o' beast...
He screw'd the pipes, and gart them skirl,
Till roof and rafters a' did dirl.

Robert Burns (1759-1796)

I will try to follow you on the last day of the world,
And pray I may see you all standing shoulder to shoulder
With Patrick Mor Macrimmon and Duncan Ban
    Macrimmon in the centre...
And you playing: 'Farewell to Scotland, and the rest of the
    earth'

Hugh MacDiarmid (1892-1978)

'... so far from the clubhouse'

They christened their game golf because they were
Scottish and revelled in meaningless Celtic noises in
the back of the throat.

Stephen Fry (born 1957)

All I've got against it is that it takes you so
far from the clubhouse.

Eric Linklater (1899-1974)
on golf

To hit a very small ball into an even smaller hole, with
weapons singularly ill designed for the pupose.

Winston Churchill (1874-1965)
on golf

Yet the finest golfers are also the least loquacious. It
is said of the illustrious Sandy McHoots that when,
on the occasion of his winning the British Open
Championship, he was interviewed by the leading daily
papers as to his views on Tariff Reform, Bimetallism,
The Trial by Jury System, and the Modern Craze for
Dancing, all they could extract from him was the single
word 'Mphm'.

P.G. Wodehouse (1881-1975)

It's not whether *you* win or lose –
but whether *I* win or lose.

Sandy Lyle (born 1958)

St Andrews Links

DANGER
Golf in progress look before crossing. When safe please cross quickly.

Safety notice at St Andrews

A golfer needs a loving wife to whom he can describe the day's play through the long evening.

P.G. Wodehouse (1881-1975)

Would you like to see a city given over
Soul and body to a tyrannising game?
If you would there's little need to be a rover,
For St Andrews is the abject city's name.

R.F. Murray (1863-1894)

Ullapool Port

Wisdom of the Scots

I know heaps of quotations, so I can always make a fair show of knowledge.

O. Douglas (1877-1948)

Don't quote your proverb until you bring your ship into port.

From the Gaelic

Here stand my books, line upon line,
They reach the roof, and row by row,
They speak of faded tastes of mine,
And things I did, but do not, know.

Andrew Lang (1844-1912)

Beauty in things exists in the mind which contemplates them.

David Hume (1711-1776)

A place for everything, and everything in its place.

Samuel Smiles (1812-1904)

Never give your reasons, for your judgment will probably be right, but your reasons almost certainly will be wrong.

Lord Mansfield (1705-1793)

For when I dinna clearly see
I always own I dinna ken;
And that's the way wi' wisest men.

Allan Ramsay (1686-1758)

I don't pretend to understand the Universe. It's a great deal bigger than I am.

Thomas Carlyle (1795-1881)

Never argue – repeat your assertion.

Robert Owen (1771-1858)

The less we speak of our intentions, the more chance there is of realising them.

John Ruskin (1819-1900)

He that has a secret should not only hide it, but hide that he has something to hide.

Thomas Carlyle (1795-1881)

Pipe band member

We often discover what will do, by finding out what will not do; and probably he who never made a mistake never made a discovery.

Samuel Smiles (1812-1904)

A fool may ask more than a wise man can answer.

Anonymous

The most imaginative men always study the hardest and are the most thirsty for new knowledge.

John Ruskin (1819-1900)

He was a bold man who first swallowed an oyster.

King James VI (1566-1625)

All great and living architecture has been the direct expression of the needs and beliefs of man at the time of its creation, and now if we would have good architecture created, this should still be so... It is absurd to think it is the duty of the modern architect to make believe he is living four, five, six hundred, or even one thousand years before.

Charles Rennie Mackintosh (1868-1928)

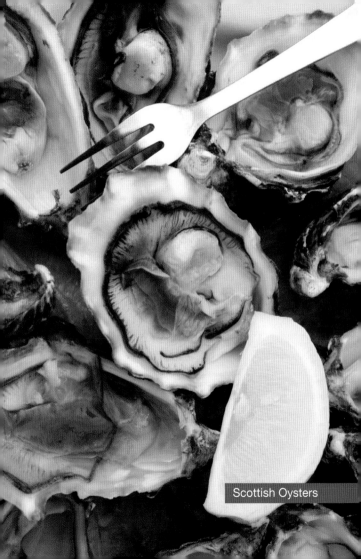

Scottish Oysters

Highland Cattle

It is the lone worker who makes the first advance in a subject: the details may be worked out by a team, but the prime idea is due to the enterprise, thought and perception of an individual.

Sir Alexander Fleming (1881-1955)

The cow – there is a thing of beauty… The eyes of a cow shine with a soft enraptured light, like moons in a misty sky…the cow lives in a deep, philosophic calm, she has long thoughts, and keeps them to herself.

John R. Allan

I am never satisfied that I have handled a subject properly 'til I have contradicted myself at least three times.

John Ruskin (1819-1900)

A bag of gravel is a history to me, and…will tell wondrous tales…mind, a bag of gravel is worth a bag of gold.

James Hutton (1726-1797)

People of the same trade seldom meet together, even for merriment and diversion, but the conversation ends in a conspiracy against the public, or in some contrivance to raise prices.

Adam Smith (1723-1790)

If your programme is to achieve artistic success (and artistic success must be the first aim) then every object you produce must have a strong mark of individuality, beauty, and outstanding workmanship.

Charles Rennie Mackintosh (1868-1928)

Industry without art is brutality.

John Ruskin (1819-1900)

There is no quite good book without a good morality, but the world is wide, and so are morals.

Robert Louis Stevenson (1850-1894)

Every person of importance ought to write his own memoirs, provided he has honesty enough to tell the truth.

Tobias Smollett (1721-1771)

Let his loyalty and devotion be a lesson to us all.

Inscription to Greyfriars Bobby

A well-written life is almost as rare as a well-spent one.

Thomas Carlyle (1795-1881)

Greyfriars Bobby

Forth Rail Bridge

I fear I have nothing original in me –
Excepting original sin.

Thomas Campbell (1777-1844)

So little done. So much to do.

Alexander Graham Bell (1847-1922)

A man's mind is a mirk mirror.

Anonymous

When you can measure what you are speaking about, and explain it in numbers, you know something about it.

Lord Kelvin (1824-1907)

Lord Kelvin – being Scotch, he didn't mind damnation, and he gave the sun and the whole solar system only ninety million more years to live.

Stephen Leacock (1869-1944)

No testimony is sufficient to establish a miracle, unless the testimony be of such a kind that its falsehood would be more miraculous than the fact which it endeavours to establish.

David Hume (1711-1776)

Highland Deer

We are often unable to tell people what they need to know, because they want to know something else.

George MacDonald (1824-1905)

Custom, then, is the great guide of human life.

David Hume (1711-1776)

That action is best, which procures the greatest happiness for the greatest numbers.

Francis Hutcheson (1694-1746)

Walter Scott Monument

Heroes of Scotland

In the garb of old Gaul, wi' the fire of old Rome,
From the heath-covered mountains of Scotia we
come.

Henry Erskine (1710-1767)

Front, flank and rear, the squadrons sweep
To break the Scottish circle deep.
That fought around their king…
The stubborn spearmen still made good
Their dark impenetrable wood,
Each stepping where his comrade stood,
The instant that he fell.

Sir Walter Scott (1771-1832)

Seeing that impossible it is, but that either I shall
offend God or else that I shall displease the world, I
have determined to obey God, notwithstanding that
the world shall rage thereat.

John Knox (1505-1572)

This that Knox did for his nation, I say, we may really
call a resurrection from death.

Thomas Carlyle (1795-1881)

What Knox really did was to rob Scotland of all the benefits of the Renaissance.

Edwin Muir (1887-1959)

There is a group of respectable Arabs, and as I come nearer I see the white face of an old man among them. He has a cup with a gold band round: his dress is a short jacket of red blanket cloth; and his pants – well, I didn't observe. I am shaking hands with him. We raise our hats, and I say, "Dr Livingstone, I presume?" and he says, "Yes".

H.M. Stanley (1841-1904)

Spirit long shaping for sublime endeavour,
A sword of God, the gleaming metal came
From stern Scotch ancestry, where whatsoever
Was true, was pure, was noble, won acclaim.

Katherine Lee Bates (1859-1929)

Gin danger's there, we'll thole our share
Gie's but the weapons, we've the will,
Ayont the main, to prove again,
Auld Scotland stands for something still.

Charles Murray (1864-1941)

John Knox's House

'In our awn land...'

For it is not glory, it is not riches, neither is it honour,
but it is liberty alone that we fight and contend for,
which no honest man will lose but with his life.

Declaration of Arbroath (1320)

For we have three great avantages;
The first is, we have the richt,
And for the richt ilk man suld ficht,
The tother is, they are comin here…
To seek us in our awn land…
The thrid is that we for our livis
And for our childer and our wifis
And for the fredome of our land
Are strenyeit in battle for to stand.

John 'The Bruce' Barbour (c. 1320-1395)

My blessing with the foxes dwell,
For that they hunt the sheep so well!
Ill fa' the sheep, a grey-faced nation
That swept our hills with desolation.

Duncan Ban MacIntyre (1724-1812)

The princesses will not leave without me. I will not
leave without their father, and the King will not leave
under any circumstances whatsoever.

Queen Elizabeth (1900-2002)
Speaking in 1940

"I will go tomorrow," said the king.
"You will wait for me," said the wind.

From the Gaelic

The waves have some mercy, but the rocks have no mercy at all.

From the Gaelic

It's no fish ye're buying; it's men's lives.

Sir Walter Scott (1771-1832)

He either fears his fate too much,
Or his deserts are small,
That puts it not unto the touch,
To win, or lose, it all.

Marquis of Montrose (1612-1650)

Happy the people whose annals are blank in the history books.

Thomas Carlyle (1795-1881)

One crowded hour of glorious life
Is worth an age without a name.

Sir Walter Scott (1771-1832)

Kirkwall Harbour

In the simplest terms, a leader is someone who knows where he wants to go, and gets up and goes.

John Erskine (1879-1951)

This is the valour of my ancestors.

A motto of Clan MacLennan

Thou shalt want ere I want.

Motto of Lord Cranstoun

Touch not the cat bot a glove.

Motto of Clan MacPherson

Furth fortune and fill the fetters.

Motto of Murray of Atholl

Grip Fast.

Motto of the Leslies

E'en do, and spare nought.

Motto of Clan MacGregor

'... the valour of my ancestors '

Gang warily.

Motto of Drummond of Perth

I bide my time.

Motto of Campbell of Loudoun

They say. What say they? Let them say.

Motto of Keith, Earl Marischal

Come hither, come hither,
You shall get flesh, you shall get flesh.
Come sons of dogs, you shall get flesh,
You shall get flesh.

War cry of Clan Cameron from the Gaelic

What is thine shall be mine.

A motto of Clan Grant

Whither will ye.

Motto of Stewart of Appin

In my end is my beginning.

Motto of Queen Mary I of Scotland (1542-1587)

It will end as it began: it came with a lass and it will go with a lass.

James V (1513-1542)

She had the face, mind and morals of a well-intentioned but hysterical poodle.

Lewis Grassic Gibbon (1901-1935)
on Mary Queen of Scots

Let the piper play 'Return No More.'

Rob Roy MacGregor (1671-1734)
last words

Scottish Wit

I love my country – every inch of it. And if it were not inhabited by my fellow-countrymen,
I'd love it even more.

Anonymous

It is never difficult to distinguish between a Scotsman with a grievance and a ray of sunshine.

P.G. Wodehouse (1881-1975)

Why should we shut our een against tomorrow
Because our sky was clouded yesterday?

James Logie Robertson (1846-1922)

One often yearns
For the land of Burns.
The only snag is
The haggis.

Lils Emslie

Let me have my own way exactly, and a sunnier and pleasanter creature does not exist.

Thomas Carlyle (1795-1881)

Wallace Monument

We all know that Prime Ministers are wedded to the truth, but like other wedded couples, they sometimes live apart.

Saki [H.H. Munro] 1870-1916

On Waterloo's ensanguined plain
Lie tens of thousands of the slain,
But none by sabre or by shot
Fell half so flat as Walter Scott.

Thomas, Lord Erskine (1750-1823)
on Scott's 'The Field of Waterloo'

Sir William Wallace – In times of peace, meek as a monk was he,
Whar weir approachit, the richt Ector was he.

Blind Harry (c. 1440-1492)

The Creator, if he exists, has a specific preference for beetles.

J.B.S. Haldane (1892-1964)

Here lies Martin Elginbrodde,
Have mercy on my soul, O Lord,
As I wad do, gin I were God,
And Ye were Martin Elginbrodde.

From a tombstone

Hearts of gold and hearts of lead
Sing it yet in sun and rain,
"Heel and toe from dawn to dusk,
Round the world and home again."

John Davidson (1857-1909)

One's prime is elusive. You little girls, when you grow
up, must be on the alert to recognise your prime, at
whatever time of life it may occur.

Muriel Spark (1918-2006)

On a Schoolmaster
Here lie Willie Michie's banes:
O Satan, when ye tak' him
Gie him the schooling of your weans,
For clever de'ils he'll mak 'em.

Robert Burns (1759-1796)

Good gracious, you've got to educate him first. You
can't expect a boy to be vicious until he's been to a
really good school.

Saki [H.H. Munro] 1870-1916

Join a Highland regiment, my boy. The kilt is an
unrivalled garment for fornication and diarrhoea.

John Masters (1914-1983)

Burns Statue

This dress is called the quelt, and for the most part, they wear the petticoat so very short that in a windy day, going up a hill, or stooping, the indecency of it is plainly discovered.

Edward Burt (*d.* 1755)

It is the restriction placed on vice by our social code which makes its pursuit so peculiarly agreeable.

Kenneth Grahame (1859-1932)

To a shower of gold most things are penetrable.

Thomas Carlyle (1795-1881)

It is not that I am idle in my nature, but propose me one thing, and it is inconceivable the desire I have to do something else.

Sir Walter Scott (1771-1832)

Oh, it's nice to get up in the mornin',
And nicer to stay in bed.

Sir Harry Lauder (1870-1950)

There is no duty we so much underrate as that of being happy.

Robert Louis Stevenson (1850-1894)

It is not by any means certain that a man's business is the most important thing he has to do.

Robert Louis Stevenson (1850-1894)

Monkeys very sensibly refrain from speech, lest they should be set to earn their living.

Kenneth Grahame (1859-1932)

Hauf his soul a Scot maun use
Indulgin' in illusions;
And hauf in gettin' rid o' them,
And comin' to conclusions.

Hugh MacDiarmid (1892-1978)

There is more knavery among kirkmen than honesty among courtiers.

Anonymous

Herein is not only a great vanity, but a great contempt of God's good gifts, that the sweetness of men's breath, being a good gift of God, should be wilfully corrupted by this stinking smoke.

King James VI (1566-1625)
'A Treatise Against Tobacco'

The Saltire Flag

I consider the world as made for me, not me for the world. It is my maxim therefore to enjoy it while I can, and let futurity shift for itself.

Tobias Smollett (1721-1771)

I am a jingo patriot of planet Earth.
"Humanity, right or wrong!"

Lewis Grassic Gibbon (1901-1935)

A general goodnight.

Thomas Chalmers (1780-1847)
last words

Acknowledgements

The publisher would like to thank the following for permission to reproduce work in copyright:

p 4 © istockphoto.com/JPStrickler
p 6 © Steve Cadman
p 8 © Gary Denham
p 10 © Jeffrey Woodgate
p 13 ©istockphoto.com/BMPix
p 14 © istockphoto.com/NickR
p 18 © istockphoto.com/davidp
p 22 © Alison Bremner
p 26 © William Marnoch
p 29 © Katherine Ingham
p 30 © Tim Rogers
p 32 © istockphoto.com/generacionx
p 36 © Peter Guthrie
p 38 © istockphoto.com/rkotulan
p 42 © Cesar G. Soriano
p 44 © Darren Greaves
p 46 © istockphoto.com/garyforsyth
p 48 © David Watterson
p 50 © David C. Elliott
p 52 © Eddie Truman
p 54 © Martin Luechinger
p 56 © Kevin Walsh
p 59 © Keith Dumble
p 61 © istockphoto.com/kayglobal

p 62 © Pete Birkinshaw
p 65 © Mark Ferbert
p 66 © istockphoto.com/texasmary
p 68 © Chris Barker
p 70 © Chris Sansenbach
p 73 © Paul Kentish
p 74 © Alan J. Stuart
p 77 © Adrian Powter
p 79 © Andrea D'Ippolito
p 82 © Tracey Paterson
p 84 © Gary Denham
p 87 © David Capes
p 90 © Amber Northfield

Other books by Appletree Press:

The Scottish Toast Master
Charles MacLean

The 'toast' is a long-established Scottish drinking tradition. This attractive guide will help you celebrate an important aspect of Scotland's social history. The custom of the 'Grace Cup' was a way of keeping restless Scots at the table until Grace was pronounced: a cup of wine passed round the table, but only after 'Grace'. The word 'toast' is derived from the eighteenth-century custom of floating toasted bread in wine. Guests proposing toasts to each other became something of an art form, often becoming an excuse for intemperate drinking at parties! This fun guide will steer you through the rules and history, providing an excellent excuse for a party to try these toasts and graces for yourself!

ISBN: 978-1-84758-009-2

Scottish Malt Guide
Derek Cooper

The *Scottish Malt Guide* is a look at the whisky distilling tradition of Scotland. The tradition stretches far back into Scottish folklore, when it was known as uisge beatha, the water of life. Since then, much has changed, but the recent revival of interest in Scottish malts shows that the desire to unravel the mysteries of their unique character still lives on. The *Scottish Malt Guide* provides an introduction to the history and working of 24 of the best-known distilleries and includes a tour of Speyside.

The *Scottish Malt Guide* is a mine of information, beautifully illustrated with colour photographs and accompanied by a variety of quotations from famous whisky lovers througout the years. This compact guide to Scottish Malts will take you on a journey to an appreciation of one of the world's most complex and distinguished drinks.

ISBN: 978-1-84758-006-1

The Scottish Kitchen
Paul Harris and Marion Maxwell

The Scottish Kitchen offers everyone a warm welcome.
A wide selection of traditional Scottish fayre is on offer
– such riches as Venison, Pheasant, Grouse and of
course Salmon. But aside from these luxury dishes there
are more simple culinary delights such as Porridge,
Herrings in Oatmeal and the ever-popular Stovies.
The Scottish baking tradition is also covered, from
breakfast to dessert, savoury or sweet, with homely
recipes for Oatcakes, Shortbread, Bannocks and
Scones. Or how about some teatime favourites such
as Dundee Cake, Apple Tart or Boiled Fruit Cake?
With attractive colour photographs throughout, these
recipes will appeal – no matter what your taste.

ISBN: 978-1-84758-007-8